CARD GAMES
FOR
ONE OR TWO

Contributing Writer:
David Galt

PUBLICATIONS INTERNATIONAL, LTD.

David Galt is a games creator, collector, teacher, and writer whose articles have appeared in *Games* magazine, *The Playing Card,* and *Games Times.* His own game creations include Intense Bridge, and his collection features many antique playing cards and board games.

Cover Illustration: Rich Lo

CONTENTS

WELCOME TO CARD GAMES

Playing cards have been around for more than 600 years, entertaining and enticing people of all ages and walks of life. Games using playing cards have come and gone over the decades and the centuries. Some games that are still played today—such as Cribbage and Casino—have roots going very far back. Others have probably already seen their glory days.

Card games remain wonderful recreations, filled with nostalgia, fun, and suspense. Whether you already play cards or not, this book is sure to bring you something new.

We're concentrating on games for one or two; excellent games for more than two players, such as Bridge, have been omitted. We have also not included games essentially of gambling interest, such as Blackjack, Chemin de Fer, and Poker. We chose for this book the best and most popular games that have endured for the last 100 years. Some have their own special vocabulary; this adds to their charm.

Look in the section on solitaire for pastimes with cards to while away an idle moment. You'll find a few games you're not familiar with. We've culled these games from among the many hundreds of solitaire games devised over the past 150 years.

In giving directions to these card games, we've assumed you have some knowledge of what a deck of cards consists of. For small matters—misdeals and dropped cards, for instance—we urge you to adhere to the general rules of good sportsmanship. In playing the games, feel free to make your own rule if one is not stated (for example, for choosing a dealer). The glossary should prove handy for defining useful and important card-game terms.

Happy shuffling!

GAMES FOR
Two

Many card games fall into families. The big Rummy family asks the player to form combinations of cards and then play them in groups called melds. Games from the Rummy family in this book are Rummy, Gin Rummy, and Canasta. Euchre and Nap are both trick-taking games in which the object is to take three out of a possible five tricks. Hearts for Two and Whistlet are versions of four-handed trick-taking games. Pinochle, Klaberjass, and Sixty-six are members of a family in which certain combinations of cards count points. Spite and Malice is actually a form of solitaire for two. Some excellent games—such as Cribbage and Casino—are in a class by themselves.

⊰ RUMMY ⊱

The exact origin of the game Rummy, as well as the reason for its name, are both remarkably unclear. Noted authors have tracked it back variously to American Whiskey Poker, Mexican Conquian, and even to a Chinese game. Rummy's initial popularity dates from America's westward expansion. It has since spawned a huge number of variants and spin-offs, including Gin Rummy, Michigan Rummy, and Canasta. Originally intended for as many as six players, Rummy has become a two-player favorite as well.

Object: To acquire "Rummy"—a hand of seven cards arranged into one three-card meld and one four-card meld. A meld may be three or four cards of the same rank or three or four cards in sequence, all of the same suit.

Sample melds in Rummy

The cards: A regular pack of 52 cards is used. Aces are low.

To play: Deal seven cards to each player, one at a time. Then place the remainder of the pack face down to form the stock. Nondealer begins by drawing the top card from the stock and discarding any card, thereby starting a face-up discard pile.

The dealer then either picks up the discard or draws the top card from the stock. Dealer then discards. The two players continue alternately, taking the top discard if it fits in with the cards in their hand or drawing a card from the stock, and then discarding. Save cards that bring your hand closer to a Rummy hand, and discard those that don't. Play continues until one player announces "Rummy," or until just two cards remain in the stock.

Scoring: If you go Rummy, you score the total count of unmatched cards opponent holds. Cards score the number of their spots; face cards score 10. If neither player goes Rummy, whoever has the lower total score in unmelded cards wins the point difference. Game may be played to 50 points or to any other agreed-upon number.

Rummy hand

Opponent's hand

7

In the example on page 7, the player with the top hand went Rummy. The second player's unmatched cards are the ◆5 and 6, which count 11, and the jack, which counts 10. The first player scores a total of 21 points for the hand.

Tips: Don't hang on to a high-scoring card if you have nothing to go with it. The winning player in the example scored 10 points from loser's unmatched jack.

In going for a three-card meld, look for card combinations that can be filled in the most ways. For example, only one card fills ◆4-◆6-♣5, only two cards can fill ◆4-◆6-◆8, but any of four cards can turn ◆4-◆5-♣5 into a meld.

Remember the cards your opponent picks up from the discard pile. Try not to discard another card for the same meld.

Keep track of all the cards played. This will allow you to make safer discards and stop you from going for a meld requiring cards already out of play.

Variations: Some players may feel more comfortable turning the first stock card up, allowing nondealer and then dealer the option of picking up that card.

Knock Rummy is a variation that permits either player to "knock" in turn, before drawing a new card. Just say the word "knock" or rap the table. Both players immediately show their hands, scoring as follows: As knocker, you win 1 game point if the count of opponent's unmatched cards is no lower than yours. You win 3 game points if you go Rummy. You win 6 game points if you go Rummy before drawing a card, or if you have Rummy with a seven-card sequence in one suit. Opponent wins 2 game points by having a count of unmatched cards lower than yours.

Tip: 45 is the total count, on average, for seven cards (assuming no melds). Therefore, if you have under 35 before play begins, you have a good chance to win a game point by an immediate knock. But keep in mind that you lose 2 game points when your count is beaten.

⊰GIN RUMMY⊱

First introduced in 1899, Gin Rummy has become the most popular two-handed card game of all time. After Hollywood discovered it in the late '30s, Gin Rummy clubs started springing up all over the United States. In the game's heyday, you couldn't find an empty table at many of these clubs.

Object: To match the cards you hold into melds of three cards or more. (See the rules for Rummy for types of melds.)

The cards: A regular pack of 52 cards is used. Aces are low.

To play: Deal ten cards to each player, one at a time. Turn the next card face up to begin a discard pile; then place the rest of the pack face down beside this upcard to form the stock.

Nondealer begins play by taking this upcard (and then discarding a card) or by declining it. If nondealer declines it, dealer may take the upcard or also decline it. If both decline the upcard, nondealer takes the top card from the stock and then discards any card.

Once play starts, the two players continue alternately, taking the top discard if it fits in with the cards in their hand or drawing a card from the stock, and then discarding a card.

Knocking: A player "knocks" by discarding face down and claiming "Knock." The player then lays down the hand in melds, with the "deadwood" (unmatched cards) separate. You can knock only if the total of your unmatched cards is less than 10 (see "Scoring"). Opponent then has the chance to lay off any deadwood on your melds. Melding all ten cards in your hand is called Gin. If you Gin, opponent can't lay off deadwood on your melds.

The winner of one hand deals the next.

When the stock is down to its final two cards, play ceases and the deal is thrown in.

Scoring: Cards count their face value, with face cards worth 10 points each. For Gin, score 25 points plus the value of all unmatched cards in your opponent's hand. For knocking, score the point value of your deadwood subtracted from opponent's deadwood after laying off.

Undercut (or underknock): Whenever opponent's remaining deadwood is less than or equal to knocker's, then opponent scores a 25-point bonus for the undercut, plus the point difference, if any.

The first player to reach 100 points wins the game.

Tips: Remember which cards have already been played. (Unless you decide otherwise, no player is allowed to look through the discards.) Especially remember the cards your opponent has picked up.

The first player "knocks" with 4, the value of the unmatched ♦4. The second player melds ♣3-4-5-6 and the three 8s. The second player also lays off deadwood by adding the ♥Q-K to the ♥9-10-J run.

Your opponent will be watching the cards you pick up. Even when you're desperate to make matches, don't pick up a discard unless it melds for you—or at least gives you great chances.

It might pay to keep a card drawn from stock that just increases your melding chances or lowers your count, if by keeping it you can discard a high card or a "safe" card (one not wanted by opponent).

Try to keep cards that you can turn easily into melds. For example, ◆8-◆9-♠9 can use any of four cards to make a meld, whereas ◆9-◆J-◆K can be improved with only two cards, ◆10 or ◆Q.

High cards are usually safest to discard early in the play. Late in the game, even a high-card pair—like two queens—is a doubtful asset. They may become "isolated" from the rest of your cards, and your opponent who finds a late queen in the stock pile may decide to keep it rather than discard it.

Take notice when your opponent discards low cards early. It may mean he or she already has a high-card meld—or is still speculating on one.

The best policy for knocking is to do it as soon as possible. Don't be timid. Holding off a few turns to play for a Gin hand will often let your opponent get rid of some dead-wood—or even make a hand better than your own—while yours doesn't improve.

Variations: Traditionally, when an ace is turned for the upcard, players must play for Gin only. Also, if the upcard is a spade, scores for that deal double. By agreement before-hand, players may adopt either rule or both.

⊰ CANASTA ⊱

Canasta is Spanish for "basket." At times you might wish you had one to hold all the cards in your hand! Though it's called the "Great Argentinean Rummy Game," Canasta actually got its start in Uruguay. It was all the rage in the United States in the early '50s. It's still a rough-and-tumble two-handed game, and it can also be played three-handed or four-handed as a partnership game. The rules are slightly different for those versions.

Object: To score points by melding, with the goal of scoring two canastas and then "going out."

The cards: Two 52-card decks including the four jokers are used.

Melding: A meld must consist of at least three cards, all of the same rank, which are placed on the table face up. Melds can be built upon in later turns so as to form canastas.

Natural canasta

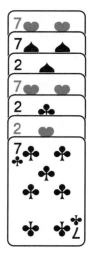

Mixed canasta

A canasta is a meld of seven cards of the same rank; it scores bonus points. Some of the seven cards can be wild cards, which can stand for any card in a meld. All jokers and deuces are wild. A "natural" canasta is composed of seven cards of the same rank and has no wild cards. A "mixed" canasta has at least four natural cards and must contain no more than three wild cards. Thus a mixed canasta of 7s will have at least four 7s and no more than three wild cards. A meld shorter than a canasta must contain at least two natural cards.

The treys: Red 3s are not used in play; they are bonus cards worth 100 points each. You lay down a red 3 as soon as you acquire it. If you manage to get all four red 3s, your bonus doubles to 800 points.

Black 3s are used in play, but they cannot be melded unless you are going out in that turn. They function as stopper cards (see "Freezing the pack").

The play: Deal 15 cards to each player, one at a time, with the remaining cards forming a stock. Then turn over an upcard to begin the discard pile, or "pack." If the upcard is a wild card or a red 3, turn another card up on top of it. (See "Freezing the pack.")

Nondealer places any red 3s on the table and replaces each one with a new card from the stock. Under rare circumstances, nondealer even may take up the upcard (see "Taking the pack"). Otherwise, nondealer draws a card from stock and may meld (equally rare at the first play), and then discards onto the pack.

Players alternate turns from then on, usually drawing and discarding.

Initial melds: Each card has a point value for melding.

Joker	50
Deuce	20
Ace	20
King through 8	10
7 through 4	5
Black 3s	5

60 points   *55 points*

Your first meld of the game must total a minimum value of 50 points. To calculate the value of a meld, simply add up the value of the cards it contains.

As long as your score is under 1500 points, you need only 50 points to meld. On later deals, if your score is between 1500 and 2995, your first meld must value at least 90. If your score is over 3000 points, your first meld must value at least 120.

Once you have made your initial meld, you can add cards to your melds that are already on the table, or make new melds, before discarding to end your turn, and:

Taking the pack: You can pick up the entire discard pile to add to your hand under these circumstances:

1. You have already melded the required minimum or can do so on this turn, and:

2. You can match the top discard with two cards of the same rank (meld the three cards on this turn), or the top discard matches cards you have already melded on the table.

Taking the pack means getting all the discards. If you are making your initial meld of the hand, only the top discard may be used to meet the initial meld count. The remaining points must come from your hand.

14

*Many cards are in the discard pile, and you distinctly remember a king.
You decide it would be worth your while to pick up the pack. You can do so by
combining the 8 on the top of the pack with the two 8s in your hand. Meld
those three cards and add the remaining cards to your hand. You can lay
down other melds you find in the pack—including the king that you
remember—but it's not required.*

Freezing the pack: Discarding a black 3 prevents your opponent from picking up the pack on that turn, since black 3s can't be melded until the end.

Discarding a wild card (a deuce or a joker) "freezes" the pack. Ordinarily you can pick up a pack if the top discard matches a meld you have on the table. To pick up a frozen pack, you must match the top discard with a natural pair in your hand. This rule applies to both players, regardless of who froze the pack initially.

15

When freezing the pack, discard the wild card sideways so that subsequent discards won't obscure it. (See illustration on page 17.) This reminds the two players that the pack is frozen. Turning over a red 3 as the first upcard also freezes the pack.

Going out: The deal ends when one player goes out—ends the play with no cards left in his hand. In order to go out, you must have completed two canastas. You meld all the cards in your hand except for one card, which must be discarded. (In some variations no final discard is necessary.)

You can add either wild cards or natural cards to already completed canastas. You can also meld black 3s as part of going out.

If all the cards in the stock have been drawn and neither player can go out, the hand ends.

Scoring: No scores are recorded until the hand ends. Then each player's score is calculated as follows:

Bonus for going out	100
Going out from concealed hand (without having previously melded)	100
Each red trey	100
Four red treys	800
Each natural canasta	500
Each mixed canasta	300

Add the values of all the cards melded, including canastas. Subtract the card values of any cards left in your hand.

Game is 5000 points. It usually takes several hands for one player to reach game. If both players go over 5000, the higher score wins.

Tips: The player who takes the pack first is likely to have a substantial edge throughout the whole hand. If the pack is large enough, it will yield some leftover cards to keep in hand for taking the pack again. It may be worth the risk or sacrifice of wild cards to steer the pack your way.

If the pack is frozen, don't add to your melds on the table with cards you draw. Remember, you must have a natural pair in your hand to pick up a frozen pack. If you have melded three jacks and later you draw two more, keep them in your hand in case your opponent decides a jack would be a safe discard.

Don't concentrate on getting natural canastas; the bonus is not enough to make a difference. The same is true for the bonus for going out with a hidden hand. You should work on getting a big score by making lots of melds.

Variations: A very common variation is to draw two cards at each turn and discard one. The pick-two-and-discard-one method of play allows both players' hands to expand in size. This gives the player who doesn't pick up the pack a better chance to remain competitive.

The wild card freezes the pack; even though you have melded kings, you can't pick up this pack unless you have two kings in your hand.

⊰ CONCENTRATION ⊱

A game of memory and attention that can be learned in 30 seconds,
Concentration is often one of the first card games a child learns. It's a good
two-handed game for players of any age, and it can be expanded to include
the whole family. Don't be surprised if the youngest participants outplay
their elders! In England, this game is called Pelmanism, after the Pelman
Institute of Education, founded in 1899.

Object: To gather in the most cards by matching them in pairs.

The cards: A regular pack of 52 cards is used.

To play: You'll need a large surface area. Deal the whole deck out, card by card, face down. It doesn't matter if the cards are in neat rows and columns or in a haphazard arrangement.

A turn of play consists of turning over one card, then another.

If these cards match in rank, remove them from the layout and keep them. Go again, turning over two new cards.

If the two cards turned aren't the same rank, your turn ends. Return the cards to their places, face down. Try to remember the turned-up cards so that you can match them later.

Scoring: When the cards have all been taken, count them to see who has more. High scorer after three games wins.

Tips: You can get the feel for this game pretty quickly. The key to it is visual and spatial recall. If you're not sure which card to turn over, you should always go with your instincts.

Variations: At each turn, you may turn over a third card whenever the first two do not match. If still no pair is produced, return them all to their places. (When down to the final six cards, only two cards may be turned.)

DR. DAVE'S IMPROVED CONCENTRATION: Cards match if they total 11—for example a 5 and a 6, a 10 and an ace, an 8 and a 3. A face card pairs with any other face card—when they're also the same rank, your turn continues; when they're two different face cards, you keep them but your turn ends. Or you can eliminate the face cards altogether.

⊰CASINO⊱

As far back as 1797, Casino was described in books on card games. It probably leads back to the earlier Italian game Scopa, or "scoop." Though the game has quite a few details, it's easy to learn. Casino is fun to play, with lots of suspense and surprise. But playing Casino well takes real skill. A watchful eye and thoughtful technique will win you many points!

Object: To score points by taking in cards by "matching," by "combining," or by "building."

The cards: A regular pack of 52 cards is used.

To play: Deal four cards to each player and four cards face up on the table. (Any method may be used, though dealing

A Casino hand and table layout.

---

pairs is the usual custom.) Dealer keeps the rest of the pack handy. Nondealer plays a card first; players then alternate until the round is over.

You can combine the card you play with cards on the table in many possible ways.

Matching: If your card matches by rank a card on the table, you can take the pair immediately. In the layout shown on page 20, ♠J matches ♦J; the two cards are placed face down in front of you.

Face cards can be taken only in pairs—if two queens are on the table and you hold another queen, you can take only one of the queens. However, if three matching face cards are on the table and you hold the fourth, you can take all four.

Combining: If your card equals the combined sum of two or more cards on the table, you can take those cards immediately. The ♥6 and the ♣4 can be taken by the ♠10 in the hand shown.

Building: If at least one free card on the table plus the card you play totals a number of a card in your hand, announce this build number and pile up the "build" to take later. In the example shown, you could play the ♦3 onto the ♥6 and say "Building 9s." On your next turn, if opponent hasn't taken it, you can take the build with your ♣9.

Opponent can change the value of a build by playing another card. In this case, opponent can play an ace on the build and say "Building 10s." This tells you he or she has a 10 with which to take the build.

But if your 9-build were still there and if you had two 9s in your hand, on your next turn you could put one of them on top of the build and say "Still building 9s," intending to take the build with your remaining 9. This creates a double build. Players can't change the value of a double build.

Nothing prevents you from taking opponent's build; you can do so if you have the right card. On the other hand, nothing prevents your opponent from taking your build!

21

Trailing: You may also play a card by "trailing" it—placing it on the table without building it onto another card. You can't do this if you have made a build that's still on the table. You must trail a card if you can't do anything else on your turn. For strategic reasons, a player might want to trail a card onto the table even though it matches the rank of one already there.

Once you have made a build, on your next turn you must either take the build, add to the build, or make a new build. Leaving a build untaken runs the risk that opponent will take it, but you may leave a build behind as long as you can add cards to it or make another play. But you may not trail a card; you must take the build first.

After the first round of four cards, dealer deals another round of four cards each and nondealer again plays first. Continue dealing four-card rounds until the pack is depleted, with dealer announcing "last" on the last round. Whoever makes the last "take" of the last round gets any cards left on the table.

Scoring: Players count their cards and note the cards with extra value. Each deal contains 11 points:

◆10 (Big Casino)	2 points
♠2 (Little Casino)	1 point
♠A, ♣A, ♥A, ◆A	1 point each
Majority of spades (7 or more)	1 point
Majority of cards (27 or more)	3 points

(If tied at 26 cards, neither player wins these points.)

Play to 21 points, or to any other agreed number.

Tips: Keeping track of what's been played—particularly the spades and points you've taken in—is critical in Casino.

Until it's been played, a certain amount of tension revolves around the ◆10, Big Casino. As nondealer, if you have the ◆10, you risk losing it if you can't take it in.

(Dealer will probably save any 10 as the final card of the round.) Beware of building 10s when your own 10 is not the ◆10.

If you are dealt any of the four aces or the ♠2, your best chance of taking them in is through building. Test your opponent's hand with a double build. Suppose you're holding an ace, a 3, and a 6, and on the table are a 3 and a 5. You'd really like to take the ace for the point. First you play the 3 on the 3, saying "Building 6s." If opponent doesn't take it, on your next play you place your ace and the 5 to make a double build of 6s—subsequently picking up the lot with your 6.

You can often rack up more points by concentrating on winning cards and spades rather than on the Big Casino and Little Casino.

As dealer, if you are dealt a face card on the last round, you are virtually guaranteed to get last card, since you play last.

Variations: Many players like to play "sweeps"—1 point for clearing the table on one play. This adds to the strategies of play. To keep track of this centuries-old scoring method, turn one card of every sweep over and add in the points later.

ROYAL CASINO: Jacks count as 11, queens 12, and kings 13. Aces may be played as either 1 or 14.

DRAW or CONTINUOUS CASINO: Place the pack between the players. Right after you play, draw a card from the pack to restore your hand to four cards.

CRIBBAGE

Based on the old game Noddy, Cribbage is thought to have been invented in the 17th century by Sir John Suckling. It crossed the Atlantic and became the favorite card game of Mr. and Mrs. Benjamin Franklin. Because you score points throughout the game, the traditional Cribbage board—using pegs—is a handy scoring device. However, you can use paper and pencil.

Object: To score points by forming certain card combinations, and to be first to reach 121 (or 61) points.

The cards: A regular pack of 52 cards is used. Each card has a point value equal to its rank. Aces are low and count 1. Face cards count 10.

Scoring combinations:

Any combination of cards totaling exactly 15 (aces count 1, face cards 10)	2 points
Pair: two cards of the same rank	2 points
Triplet: three cards of the same rank	6 points
Quartet: four cards of the same rank	12 points
Sequence: three or more cards in a row, any suit (aces always low)	1 point per card
Flush: four cards of the same suit	1 point per card
Jack of the "starts" suit	1 point

To play: Deal six cards each, one at a time. Both players select two cards to discard together. These cards are put face down to form a four-card "crib" belonging to the dealer.

Next, nondealer cuts the pack and dealer turns up the top card. This is the "start" card. If the start card is a jack, dealer "pegs 2" (scores 2 points).

*Nondealer, holding the hand on left, should keep the ace, the king, and the two
4s—these are combinations of 15. The 9 and the 3 go into the dealer's crib.
Dealer, holding the hand on right, keeps the sequence of Q-J-10 and the 5. The
7 and 8—still good cards because they add up to 15—go into the crib.*

Nondealer now plays any one card from hand face up, calling out its value. Dealer does the same, calling out the total of the two cards played. The two players continue back and forth in this way without exceeding 31. If you cannot play without going past 31, say "Go," which instructs your opponent to continue playing as many cards as possible without going past 31. Opponent pegs 1 for your "go" if able to play under 31. A player who reaches 31 exactly pegs 2 points. One more point is pegged by whoever plays the last card. When both players are unable to play, a new count is started by the player who did not make the most recent play.

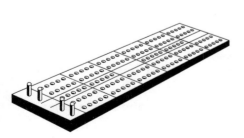

The board has 30 holes in each of the long rows, marked off in groups of five. Each player gets two pegs. In the beginning, the four pegs sit at the start end of the board. The pegs move up the outside and down the inside back to the start, for a total of 61 points. The usual game is two trips, or 121 points. The two pegs are used alternately, the back peg leapfrogging over the front peg.

25

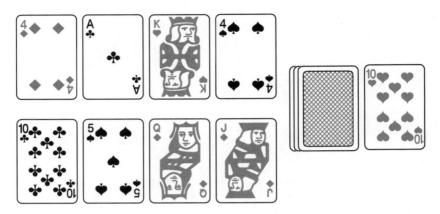

Nondealer's first play is ◆4; "Four." is called. Dealer now plays ♣10 and adds to the count, calling "14." Nondealer plays ♣A, saying "15 for 2" and pegging 2 points. This is followed by "20," "30," and "Go." Nondealer also cannot play under 31 but pegs 1 for dealer's "go." Dealer plays the queen and calls "10," starting a new count.

Pegging for melds made in play: In addition to the scoring for "go," 31, and last card, combinations made during play score points. If your play makes the count 15, score 2. If you match the rank of the card played by opponent, score 2 for the pair. Three cards of the same rank are worth 6 points, and the fourth one scores 12. Sequences also count, and the cards don't have to be in exact order. Example: 3-6-4-5 scores 4 points for the last player, and if the next player follows with a deuce, that sequence is worth 5 points. A flush (series of cards of the same suit) does not score in play; it scores only when scoring the hand. Cards must be played consecutively within one 31-count to score.

Scoring the hands: After the cards have been played out, each player's hand and dealer's crib is counted and scored. Nondealer's hand pegs first, then dealer's, then the dealer's crib. The start card is scored as a fifth card in each hand.

In the illustrated hand, nondealer is credited for each combination of cards that adds up to 15: ♥10 plus ♠4 plus ♣A; ♥K plus ♠4 plus ♣A; ♥10 plus ◆4 plus ♣A; and ♥K plus ◆4 plus ♣A. Nondealer also gets 2 points for the pair of 4s. Nondealer calls out the score and pegs it accordingly: "15-2, 15-4, 15-6, 15-8, and a pair makes 10."

Dealer pegs 16, saying, "15-2, 15-4, 15-6, 15-8, and a double run makes 16." The double run—♥10-♣10-◆J-◆Q—equals two sequences plus a pair, or 8 points.

By custom, nondealer now gathers up all the cards except the crib and the "start." Dealer then turns up the crib and pegs its score. In the crib for this hand—◆9-♣3-♥7-♣8—dealer would say, "15-2 and a four-card run makes 6."

Pegging out: As soon as one player pegs to 121 (or 61, in a shorter game), the game ends. If you win by more than 60 points (a "skunk"), score for a double game.

Tips: One of the fine arts of Cribbage is choosing which cards to go into the crib and which cards to keep. If you have a high-scoring four-card group, such as 7-8-8-9, keep them and put the other two in the crib.

If it's your own crib, put scoring cards such as pairs and 15s (or at least a 5-spot) into the crib, when this also leaves you a reasonable hand. In general, put middle-range cards (4 through 8) in your own crib, and put high and low cards (2s and kings) in your opponent's. Take into account how many start cards will be good for the various choices of cards to keep. Likewise, consider how different start cards can combine with your crib discards.

In play, start with a card that counts under 5 so that opponent can't peg an immediate 15.

Near the end of the game, scoring order can greatly influence your discards and your decisions in play. For example, if you need just 3 or 4 points to win, then you don't need a high-scoring hand. Try to keep cards that will permit you to win during the play-out.

Similarly, when dealer is 5 or 10 points from winning, opponent needs to score points soon and may have to gamble on getting help from the start card for a high-scoring hand.

❧CRAZY EIGHTS❧

Eights are wild here—hence the name—but the same game is also called
Swedish Rummy, Snooker, and just plain Eights. Since Crazy Eights is
an easy game that requires a large amount of luck, it's a good game
to play with kids.

Object: To get rid of all your cards.

The cards: A regular pack of 52 cards is used.

To play: Deal seven cards to each player. Place the rest of
the pack face down as a stock pile, but turn over the top
stock card as a "starter."

Nondealer begins by covering the starter with a matching
card of either the same rank or the same suit. After that, the
players take turns matching the top card showing. If you
can't match, draw cards from the stock until you find a
match. For example, if the starter is ♥5, nondealer can play
any heart or any 5. If nondealer plays ♣5, dealer can then
play any club or either of the remaining 5s.

All 8s are wild. You can play an 8 any time and call it any
suit (but you can't specify the rank). Opponent must match
the suit you name or play another 8.

Play until one player has no cards left. But if the stock is
gone and no one can match the top card, the game is
"blocked" and play ends.

Scoring: A player who "goes out" scores the point total
of cards left in opponent's hand. The 8s count 50, face cards
10, and all others their number values (ace = 1). In a
blocked game, both players total their points; whoever has
the lower count scores the difference. Game is to 100 points,
or any other agreed number.

Tips: If possible, when opponent has had to draw, keep playing the same suit. Use an 8 to change to that suit.

All else being equal, play a card you have a pair of. That way, if opponent matches by rank instead of by suit, you'll also have a match.

Try to remember the cards that have been played. You should at least notice when one suit has been played a lot.

Variations: In some games, you must announce "one card" when that's all you have left. If you don't say it, you are not allowed to play the card and must instead draw two cards.

An interesting variation is to give special powers to cards other than 8s. For example:

9—Wild, but you must change suit to one of a different color

5—Opponent draws 1 card

6—Play again

Ace—Starts a sequence of plays in which each player follows only with an ace or a deuce. When you play an ace say, "One." Your opponent must play either an ace or a deuce and then recite the new total. Whoever cannot add on must draw cards equal to the total reached. Example: First player plays an ace and says, "One." Second player plays a deuce and says, "Three." First player plays a deuce and says, "Five." Second player has neither an ace nor a deuce and therefore must draw five cards. Wild cards may not be used in this sequence.

Other variations specify one or more of the following: When one player plays ♠Q, the other must draw five cards; when one player plays a jack, the other loses a turn; or when a 2 is played, the next player must draw two cards.

29

⊰ SPITE AND MALICE ⊱

This engaging game is a derivative of the 19th century European game Rabouge and is a considerable improvement on Russian Bank. Spite and Malice gives plenty of chances for planning, strategy, and surprise. Promoted by Bridge greats R. F. Foster and Easley Blackwood, Spite and Malice quickly became a popular game pitting husband against wife. It won't take you long to appreciate its whimsical name.

Object: To play off all your "payoff pile" cards, or at least more of them than your opponent can.

The cards: Two 52-card decks plus their four jokers are used. Kings are high and aces are low.

To play: The two players sit across from each other. Shuffle all four jokers with one of the decks; this creates a shared draw pile. Shuffle and divide the other deck equally so that each player has a face-down 26-card payoff pile.

Each player turns up the top card of their payoff pile, and whoever shows the lower card deals a five-card hand from the draw pile to each player. Nondealer plays first.

At each turn you must play any aces you have—in hand or on your payoff pile—to the center of the table. These aces start the "center stacks."

You may make any, all, or none of the other possible plays. Play a card from your hand to begin one of four "side stacks" (start one side stack per turn, until you have four).

You can play one or more cards from your hand onto one or more of your own side stacks. Each card added must either be the same rank as the top card on the pile or else be one rank lower (any 5 on any 6).

You can move the top card from a side stack, either onto another side stack or to start a new side stack.

You can play a card from your hand, your payoff pile, or your side stacks onto the center stacks. You play a 2 on an ace, a 3 on a 2, a 4 on a 3, and so forth, upward to the king. Suit does not matter.

Before beginning your turn, draw cards from the draw pile to replace cards you've played, maintaining your hand at five cards. Keep playing until you cannot make a further play or choose not to do so. Just say, "That's it," and it's opponent's turn.

When a center stack is built up to the king, shuffle all 13 cards in with the remaining draw cards.

Jokers: A joker can stand for any card except an ace. You can play jokers onto the shared center piles or onto your own side stacks.

Bonus turns: Whenever you play all five cards from your hand at once, you get an extra turn. Take five new cards from the draw pile and keep playing.

If neither player can—or will—make a play, the game is blocked. In a blocked game, you must make any obvious plays that opponent requests.

Scoring: A player who "goes out" (plays off the whole payoff pile) scores the number of cards left in opponent's payoff pile plus a 10-point bonus. In a blocked game, whoever has fewer payoff-pile cards scores the difference, with no bonus.

Play to 25 points, or to any other agreed number.

Tips: Your immediate goal is always to try to play off your top payoff-pile card. It's well worth spending a joker or two to get to it.

A constant goal is to make things difficult for your opponent. For example, try to build center stacks just past the payoff-pile card your opponent currently has showing.

Try to start your side stacks with high cards, giving yourself more room to build downward. You can play cards of the same rank to side stacks, but it becomes harder to empty such piles. Sequential piles play right off onto center stacks.

Variations: Some versions let you play only one card in any turn to a side stack. Others follow the rule that layoffs in sequence must alternate between red and black cards.

Some players do not take a bonus turn for playing out all five cards from the hand—or else the bonus is allowed only if all five cards play into the center.

You can play a blocked game out to the end by collecting all cards except for those still in the payoff pile. Shuffle this whole bundle together, deal five cards each, and resume play.

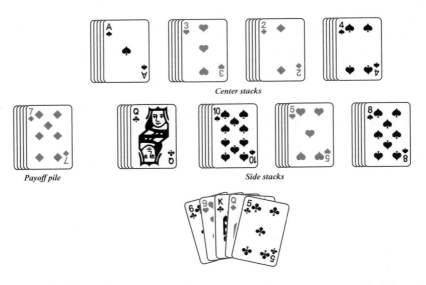

The ♥5 from the side stack can go on the ♠4 on the center stack, followed by
♣6 from the hand, ♦7 from the payoff pile, ♠8 from the side stack, ♥9 from
the hand, and ♠10 from the side stack. The ♦Q can be played onto the ♣Q on
the side stack, but the player might prefer not to do that.

⤳HEARTS FOR TWO⤲

This streamlined version for two players of the popular four-handed game retains a lot of the sport of the original version.

Object: To get the lower score. Hearts taken in tricks count 1 each, and the ♠Q taken in a trick counts 6. Or you can "shoot the moon," which means to take all of the hearts plus the ♠Q and score 19 for the other player.

The cards: A regular pack of 52 cards is used. Aces are high.

To play: Deal 13 cards to each player, one at a time. Put the remainder of the pack face down as the stock. Unlike the four-handed game, Hearts for Two does not permit exchanging cards before play. Nondealer leads to the first trick.

You must follow suit if you are able to; otherwise, play any card. No suit is trump. The trick is taken by the higher card of the suit that is led. After each trick, both players take a new card from the stock, the winner of the trick drawing first.

The traditional adage of four-handed Hearts applies: Hearts may not be led until a heart has been discarded. Of course, should you have nothing but hearts, you must play one.

Although in four-handed Hearts the rule is to discard the ♠Q at the first opportunity, the two-handed version doesn't require it. The reason for the rule when more people are playing is to forestall charges of favoritism; this complaint can't arise in a two-handed game. However, if a player leads the ♠A, opponent must follow with the queen if able to. If a player leads ♠K, opponent also must follow with the queen or else win the trick with the ace.

Play continues until all tricks have been played out, even after the stock is exhausted.

33

Point-scoring cards in Hearts for Two.

Scoring: Players count the hearts in the tricks they have taken and score a point for each. The player who took the ♠Q in a trick scores 6 points. Low score wins after ten hands. A successful moon shot scores 19 points for the other player.

Tips: You usually want to avoid taking tricks. When you win a trick, use a high card. When you lose a trick, also use a high card—for example, play the ♣10 under the ♣J.

Deuces are especially valuable, for they let you lose the lead as long as opponent can follow suit. Of course, once the deuce is played, the 3 becomes low in that suit.

If you void yourself in a suit, you can discard the ♠Q when that suit is led. As long as you have the queen, hold other spades as protection against opponent's spade leads.

If you do not have the ♠Q, and suspect that opponent may, lead spades lower than the queen.

To shoot the moon, a player will need enough high hearts to win every heart trick. Don't let opponent's hearts become too strong by discarding the wrong heart. From ♥A-10-2, discard the ♥10 and save the ♥A as insurance against a moon shot from opponent. You always have to sacrifice and win at least a heart or two to stop a moon shoot.

Variations: You may:

Count the ◆10 (some prefer the ◆J) as -5.
Require that clubs be led at the first trick.
Allow hearts to be led at any time.
Require the ♠Q to be played at the first opportunity.
Consider that playing the ♠Q does "break hearts."
Count the ♠Q as 13 and the ◆J or ◆10 as -10, which are
   their traditional values in the four-handed game.

⚓ WHISTLET ⚓

This game appears to be a compact form of "German Whist." Simple to play, Whistlet supplies an engaging mix of luck and skill. And you can learn to play this trick-taking game in about one minute.

Object: To win the most tricks.

The cards: A regular pack of 52 cards is used. Aces are high.

To play: Deal seven cards to each player, one at a time. Turn the next card over and place it next to the stock. The suit of this card will be the trump suit.

Nondealer leads to the first trick. You must follow suit when you are able to; otherwise you may trump or discard. A trick is won by the higher trump in it or, if it contains no trump, by the higher card of the suit led. After each trick, both players take a new card from the stock, the winner of the trick drawing first. The winner leads to the next trick.

Each deal consists of 26 tricks. The last seven tricks are played after the stock pile is gone. (Note that the winner of the 19th trick draws the one remaining stock card: The loser of that trick takes the trump upcard.) Keep track of individual tricks each player has won.

Scoring: The player who took the greater number of tricks scores the difference between that number and the lesser number of tricks. If both players took 13 tricks, neither scores; but if one player took 15 tricks and the other took 11 tricks, the winner scores 4 points.

Tips: Even if you are void in a suit, use judgment in trumping. It may be better strategy to shed a loser by discarding it.

In the last seven tricks, it will pay to have more trumps than your opponent.

Suppose hearts are trump. With the last seven tricks to go, you should play the top hand by leading ♥10, forcing opponent to take it with the ace. After regaining the lead, draw opponent's remaining trumps by leading a winning heart each time. Then the rest of your cards are winners, too.

The trump suit contains exactly 13 cards. If you keep count of the trumps played, you'll know in the endgame just how many trumps your opponent has.

As in most games, the better you remember the cards that have been played, the better you'll do. Keeping track of trumps and a few high cards is helpful, but if you can remember every card in the first part of the game, you'll know your opponent's last seven cards.

In the first phase of play, you may well discover opponent to be void of a suit. It may be a good risk to continue leading that suit, when your objective is to reduce your opponent's trumps. If your objective instead is to win your low trumps, then it may pay to lead a singleton, hoping to remain void in that suit later.

Variation: Play Whistlet just as above, but try to lose as many tricks as possible. When you must win a trick, use the highest card available. At the end of play, the one with fewer tricks scores the points.

⊰EUCHRE⊱

Card historians trace the roots of Euchre back to the Spanish game of Triomphe, mentioned as long ago as 1520. Euchre may have been brought to North America by French settlers in Louisiana. It was very popular 80 to 100 years ago.

Object: To win at least three of five tricks.

The cards: A 24-card deck, A-K-Q-J-10-9 for each suit. Cards rank A-K-Q-J-10-9 except in trumps, where the jack—called the "right bower"—is the highest trump, and the other jack of that color is the second highest trump—the "left bower."

To play: Deal five cards to each player, in groups of three and two, then two and three.

Dealer turns the next card up to propose trumps. Nondealer either accepts this suit as trumps and becomes the "maker," or else passes. The maker has to win at least three of the five tricks. If nondealer passes, dealer may accept the suit, becoming the maker, or pass. If both pass, nondealer may

The rank of cards in trumps.

choose a trump suit (other than the one turned up) or pass again, in which case dealer may select a suit, or pass again. When both pass twice, throw the deal in.

When the original card turned up is accepted by either player as the trump suit, dealer has the right to exchange any card in hand for it.

Nondealer always leads to the first trick. You must follow suit when you are able to; otherwise you may trump or discard. A trick is won by the higher trump in it or, if it contains no trump, by the higher card. The winner of each trick leads to the next.

The two hands shown below form an old Euchre challenge. Clubs are trumps—and the jack of spades is the left bower, the second highest trump. Although dealer (on the bottom) has four trump and nondealer has only three, nondealer can still win three tricks. If nondealer leads ♥A, dealer takes the trick with ♣10. Dealer then leads the left bower, ♠J, and nondealer takes it with ♣J. Nondealer leads ♥10, and dealer takes it with ♣Q. No matter which card dealer leads now, the remaining two tricks are nondealer's.

Scoring: If the maker wins at least three tricks, score 1 point for taking either three or four tricks. Score 2 points for taking all five tricks (a "march"). If the maker does not take at least three tricks, that player is "Euchred" and the opponent scores 2 points.

Game is played to 5 points or any other number agreed upon by the players.

Tips: You can see five cards plus the upcard. Of the 18 other cards, opponent has five. That makes the odds 13 to 5 that any given card is not in play.

Three good trumps and prospects for one more trick are usually enough for a "take." As nondealer with that kind of hand, accept the turned-up trump suit even knowing that dealer will pick that card up.

It's likely that nondealer who passes does not have good cards in the suit shown. As dealer, you'll be adding the up-card to your hand should you accept the suit and become the maker.

Variations: Euchre may be played with a 32-card pack including the 8s and 7s.

In the 1860s, a variation called Railroad Euchre added a joker as the highest trump.

Some people play that dealer is allowed to delay the exchange for the upcard until it's needed.

⊰ SIXTY-SIX ⊱

A member of the Bezique family, Sixty-six is a quiet game with good interplay. The name comes from the scoring: 130 points are in the game, so to win the hand, you need more than half—you need 66 points.

Object: To score 66 points by trick-taking and melding K-Q "marriages."

The cards: A 24-card deck of 9s through aces is used. In every suit, cards rank A-10-K-Q-J-9.

To play: Deal six cards to each player, three at a time. Turn up one card designating trumps; place it slightly under the rest of the pack.

To begin the first phase of play, nondealer leads any card and dealer plays any card. You needn't follow suit, and you may trump opponent's lead.

Each trick is won by the higher trump (if any) or else by the high card of the suit led. After each trick, both players take a new card from the stock, the winner of the trick drawing first. The winner of each trick leads to the next.

Whoever has the 9 of trumps may exchange it for the trump upcard, as long as that player has won at least one trick. However, if the 9 of trumps is the last card drawn from stock, it's not exchanged; the other player takes the upcard.

Play continues in this way until the cards have all been drawn. When only two draw cards are left, the loser of that trick takes the trump upcard.

The second phase begins after the stock is gone. Players continue to play tricks from their hands, but you must follow suit; trump or play any card if unable to follow suit.

40

Marriages: A "marriage" consists of the king and queen of the same suit (see "Scoring"). To claim a marriage on your turn, show it and then lead one of the cards.

Closing: Before the stock is gone, a player having the lead may announce, "The game is closed." The player then turns over the trump upcard. No more cards are drawn and the play advances to phase two. Marriages may still be declared.

Scoring:

Marriage in trumps	40
Marriage in another suit	20
Each ace taken in a trick	11
Each 10 taken in a trick	10
Each king taken in a trick	4
Each queen taken in a trick	3
Each jack taken in a trick	2

Taking the last trick scores 10 unless either player closed the game. A player reaching 66 or more scores 1 game point if opponent has 34 or more, 2 game points if opponent has 33 or less, and 3 game points should opponent be trickless. The first player to score 7 game points is the winner.

During play, a player can announce "66," terminating play. The remaining cards are not played or scored. If the player announcing 66 doesn't actually have 66, opponent scores 2 game points. Should the final tally show both players over 66, but with neither having announced it, neither scores.

Tips: Keep track so you can predict when you hit 66.

If you have the trump marriage, worth 40, you need only 26 other points. If all you need to win is a few tricks, close the game.

If you have high nontrump cards, you may want to close the game just to protect a good trick-taking hand.

41

⊰NAP or NAPOLEON⊱

The emperor Napoleon Bonaparte was neither the inventor nor the popularizer of this game, but his name is used for one of the bids in the game. Two of his enemies, Wellington and Blucher, are also bids.

Object: To outbid the other player and then to win the number of tricks you've bid for.

The cards: A regular pack of 52 cards is used. Aces are high.

To play: Dealer deals five cards each in groups of three and then two. Starting with nondealer, each player must make one bid, naming a number of tricks to be won. The bid does not name desired trump suit, only number of tricks.

Bids in Nap:

1	1 trick
2	2 tricks
3	3 tricks
Misère (me-ZARE)	3 tricks, no trump suit
4	4 tricks
Napoleon	5 tricks
Wellington	5 tricks
Blucher	5 tricks

A Misère bid outranks a bid of 3. Napoleon, Wellington, and Blucher are all bids to take all five tricks, but each scores differently. This means that a player who bids Napoleon for five tricks can be outbid by the other player bidding Wellington or Blucher.

42

Nondealer must bid 2 or pass. Dealer becomes the "maker" by bidding higher. If neither player bids, throw the hand in.

Maker begins by leading a card to the first trick. This card's suit becomes trump, except, of course, if the bid is Misère, which is no trump. You must follow suit when you are able to; otherwise you may trump or discard. A trick is won by the higher trump in it or, if it contains no trump, by the higher card. The winner of each trick leads to the next.

Scoring: If as maker you win the number of tricks you bid, score the number of points you bid. Nothing extra is scored for overtricks. If you bid and make Napoleon, Wellington, or Blucher, score 10 points.

The opponent scores for defeating maker's bid. If maker doesn't take the number of tricks bid, opponent scores that number. Opponent scores 5 for defeating Napoleon, 10 for defeating Wellington, and 20 for defeating Blucher. It's the risk of greater loss that separates the three different bids for all five tricks.

Nap is a fast game to play. The first to reach 30 points—or a higher number if you like—is the winner.

Either dealer or nondealer could bid 3.

Tips: Since only ten cards are in play at a time, the odds are better than eight to one against your opponent having any one particular card. Thus if you have K-Q of trump, that will win two tricks eight out of nine times on the average.

A-K-Q of trump are three easy tricks, but A-3-2 of trump will also take three tricks whenever opponent has zero or one card of the suit. Remember, you must lead a trump at the first trick, and in this case you'd lead the ace.

Bid Misère when you have three sure or probable tricks such as three aces, two aces and a king, or an ace and two kings. Also, as nondealer, bid Misère when you don't want a bid of 3 to be outbid by dealer bidding Misère. As nondealer with A-K-Q in one suit, Misère is the correct bid, since the maker—the high bidder—leads first.

A good Misère hand.

As nondealer, when you have a near-certain five easy tricks, bid Blucher rather than Napoleon, to prevent dealer from outbidding you. A Napoleon bid for nondealer would be a hand with five probable winners, or even four sure winners in trump and just about any other card. To defeat you, opponent would need five trumps—or would have to hold onto the right card to capture your last card.

A reasonable hand for Nap.

⊰ SETBACK or ⊱ AUCTION PITCH

This widely played game, also known as High-Low-Johnny, descends from 17th century England's All-Fours. Its contemporary cousins include Seven-Up, Pedro, Cinch, and California Jack.

Object: To score points by winning cards in tricks. The four points to be won are the hand holding high trump for the deal, the hand holding low trump for the deal, the trick taking the jack of trump, and "game"—the high card-count total in tricks taken.

The cards: A regular pack of 52 cards is used. Aces are high; however, 10s are the highest-scoring cards (see "Scoring").

To play: Deal six cards to each player, three at a time. The rest of the cards are not needed.

Starting with nondealer, each player bids once for the right to choose the trump suit. The possible bids are—from weakest to strongest—one, two, three, and four. Dealer, to bid, must outbid nondealer, but either one may "pass" (not bid). If both players pass, throw the cards in and deal a new hand.

High bidder designates the trump suit by leading a card of that suit to the first trick. This is the "pitch." You must follow suit if a trump card is led. If another suit is led you may play a trump even if you are able to follow suit. You may not discard, however, if you are able to follow suit. A trick is won by the higher trump in it or, if the trick contains no trump, by the higher card. The winner of each trick leads to the next.

Scoring: When the six tricks are played, score each hand.

High trump	1
Low trump	1
Jack of trumps	1
Game (high card-count total)	1
Each ace	4
Each king	3
Each queen	2
Each 10	10

The points for high and low trump card are each awarded to the player whose hand contained the card, not the player who took the card in a trick. The point for jack of trumps (if the card was present) goes to the player who took it in a trick. Whoever has taken the higher card count in tricks earns 1 point for game (in case of tie, neither wins this point).

Each player scores the number of points earned on the deal. The bidder must score at least the number bid or else is "set back" (loses) that amount. The first player to reach 11 wins (or you may agree to another number, for example 7, 13, or 21).

Tips: When you hold three or more trumps, it's unlikely that opponent has more than two. It's often wise to "draw" opponent's trumps by continuing to lead them. Remember, opponent is free to play a trump card instead of following suit.

Don't bid four without seeing the jack of trumps in your hand.

⇥ PINOCHLE ⇤

Although Auction Pinochle (the three-handed version) is perhaps the most competitive form, two-handed Pinochle was probably the most popular card game for two in the United States before the advent of Gin Rummy.

Object: To score the most points by melding and by taking tricks.

The cards: A double deck—what's known as a Pinochle deck—each deck consisting of A, K, Q, J, 10, 9 of each suit (48 cards total). The cards rank A, 10, K, Q, J, 9.

To play: Deal 12 cards to each player; turn the next card up to designate the trump suit. If it's a 9, dealer scores an immediate 10 points. The remaining cards form a stock pile.

Every deal has two phases: trick-taking with melding and the endgame. To begin the first phase, nondealer leads any card; dealer may follow by playing any card—you don't have to follow suit. Each trick is won by the higher trump, or if it contains no trump, by the higher card of the suit led. If the two cards are identical, the first one played wins. Winner of the trick may meld any one of these combinations:

Pinochle (♠Q-♦J)	40 points
♠A-♥A-♣A-♦A ("100 aces")	100 points
♠K-♥K-♣K-♦K ("80 kings")	80 points
♠Q-♥Q-♣Q-♦Q ("60 queens")	60 points
♠J-♥J-♣J-♦J ("40 jacks")	40 points
K and Q, same suit (marriage)	20 points
Marriage in trump	40 points
A-10-K-Q-J of trump (flush)	150 points
Each 9 of trump ("dix," pronounced "deece")	10 points

47

Though a player may hold more than one meld in hand, after winning a trick only one melding combination may be tabled. Another trick must be won to make the second meld. This does not apply to the 9s of trump. The first dix can be exchanged for the upcard to get a higher trump. The second is simply shown to opponent and the 10 points scored.

A melded card may be used again in a different meld. For example, the ♠Q may be melded with the ♠K in a marriage; then after winning a later trick, the same ♠Q may be melded with a ◆J in a pinochle, or with ♣Q-♥Q-◆Q for 60 queens. A second marriage in spades would require a new ♠Q and ♠K. Cards melded on the table still belong to the hand of their owner and may be played to any trick. However, cards taken in tricks are out of play for the rest of the hand.

After a trick is won and any meld tabled, both players take a new card from the stock, the winner of the trick drawing first. Winner of the trick then leads to the next trick.

A player cannot meld 40 jacks and later meld 60 queens, also claiming the 40 points for pinochle. The player should first meld the pinochle and later meld the jacks and queens.

Endgame play: When only the upcard and a single stock card are left, the winner of the trick takes the stock card, and the loser takes the upcard (which at this point will be the 9 of trump). No further melds may be made. Players return to their hands any cards melded on the table, and the winner of the last trick starts the endgame by leading any card.

In playing the tricks during the endgame, a player must follow suit if able; otherwise, the player must trump if able.

When a trump is led, opponent must play a higher trump if able. The object is to take tricks with high-scoring cards.

Scoring: After all the tricks have been played, players total up cards won as follows:

Each ace	11 points
Each 10	10 points
Each king	4 points
Each queen	3 points
Each jack	2 points
Last trick	10 points

Scorekeeper adds these trick points to each player's melds and reports the running totals. Game is usually played to 1000 points. If both players go over 1000 points on the same deal, whoever has the higher total wins.

Tips: Cards played to tricks in the first phase of the game are no longer available for melding. Play a possible melding card only if you're sure you can spare it. Win tricks with 10s, not with aces (unless you have a duplicate of that ace).

Kings and queens (especially the ♠Q) are good melding cards. Retain these cards while the possibility of melding with them is still alive. Jacks are not valuable cards to keep for melding (except the ♦J). Four different jacks score only 40 points, so unless you have this meld, don't keep jacks.

If you've seen both ♦Ks, then all other kings become less valuable, since 80 kings is no longer a possible meld.

If your opponent plays a good melding card early, it's likely to be a duplicate. However, opponent may be missing the rest of the meld and be strapped for a play.

Use a trump in beginning play to meld some cards and free them for play, or to prevent opponent from melding. In the endgame a long trump suit will bring in several extra tricks, as well as the last trick.

In the endgame, beware the singleton ace. If opponent plays the other ace, you follow suit and lose. Play yours first.

⊰ KLABERJASS ⊱

Try pronouncing this game "Klobber-yosh"—or just call it Klob. Probably Hungarian in origin, it became a favorite for gamblers in the United States as a one-on-one test of talent. Though Klaberjass is like Euchre in putting the jack atop the trump ladder, it is closer to the Bezique family. The game may seem complicated at first, but you'll pick it up after a few hands.

Object: To score points by declaring sequences and by winning high-counting cards in tricks.

The cards: A 32-card deck, A-K-Q-J-10-9-8-7 for each suit. The rank of trump cards is different from that in the other suits. Card rank in trumps: J (high), 9, A, 10, K, Q, 8, 7. Card rank in the other suits: A, 10, K, Q, J, 9, 8, 7.

Trump

Nontrump

To play: Deal six cards to each player, one at a time, and turn over an upcard to propose trump. Save the rest of the cards for further dealing.

Nondealer speaks first, saying "Pass," "Take," or "Schmeiss" (pronounced "shmice"). "Take" means nondealer accepts the suit turned up as trump, becoming the "maker," or player responsible for making the higher score. "Schmeiss" is an offer to throw the hand in. If dealer accepts, the cards are thrown in for a new deal. If dealer refuses, the schmeisser must become the maker with the upcard suit as trump. If nondealer passes, dealer then must pass, accept, or schmeiss.

50

If you both pass on the first round, nondealer names a new trump suit or passes again. If the latter, dealer now names a new trump suit or passes. If both pass twice, the hand is thrown in, with no redeal; the deal alternates in Klaberjass.

Once a suit has been settled on for trumps, each player is then dealt another three cards, bringing the hands to nine cards. At this time it's also customary to turn up the bottom card of the deck.

If the original upcard was accepted as trump, either player with the 7 of trump may now exchange it for the upcard.

Sequences: Before playing out the tricks, determine which player, if either, has the highest sequence. Only the player with the highest-ranking sequence may score for sequences. For sequences only, each suit follows the order A-K-Q-J-10-9-8-7. Three or more cards in a row, all of the same suit, form a sequence.

A three-card sequence is worth 20 points; a four-card or longer sequence is worth 50 points. A 50-point sequence is higher than a 20-point sequence. Between sequences of equal value, the one with the higher top card is higher. If the sequences tie in rank, a sequence in trump beats one not in trump. If neither is trump, nondealer's beats dealer's.

Nonmaker begins the dialogue, claiming "20" or "50" or "no sequence." Maker now answers, either declaring "no sequence," or agreeing that nonmaker's meld is "good"—or, if the sequences have equal value, by asking, "How high?"

The player whose sequence is high may also declare any other sequence, regardless of its value or rank. To score your sequences, you must show them before playing to the second trick. The other player scores no sequences.

Once the sequences dialogue is over, play begins. No matter who the maker is, nondealer always makes the first lead. Thereafter, the winner of a trick leads to the next one.

A trick is won by the higher trump in it or, if it has no trump, by the higher card. You must follow suit if able. If unable to follow suit, you must trump if possible; otherwise, you may discard. If a trump is led, you must play a higher trump if able.

As nondealer, with this hand, you could take hearts and probably win, but clubs would also be good as trumps. Pass now, giving opponent a chance to take or schmeiss. If opponent passes, you can name clubs on the second round.

Bella: If you hold the K-Q of trump, declare 20 points for "Bella" when you play the second of them to a trick.

Scoring: Each player earns points by taking certain cards in tricks.

Jack of trump ("Jass," pronounced "yahss")	20
9 of trump ("Menel," pronounced "muh-NIL")	14
Each ace	11
Each 10	10
Each king	4
Each queen	3
Each jack (not trump)	2
Last trick	10

Players combine this score with any melds or Bella. If maker's total is more than defender's, then both record their points. If maker and defender tie, defender's score only is recorded. If defender scores more than maker, credit defender with both scores. First player to 500 points wins.

Tips: You won't always have a rock-crusher of a hand in the first six cards. The last three cards received can be high trumps and nice cards for sequences, or useless losers, or a mix of the good and the bad. If you become the maker needing to fill in an open sequence, you probably won't get it. With two sequences open, your chances improve a good deal.

J-Q-K or J-9-A of trump is an obvious "take," but you may want to take with J-Q of trump plus some high tricks. Jack alone with two outside tricks is a very reasonable take. Also, to accept with A-K-Q of trump (40 points with Bella) and an outside ace will usually win—unless opponent has very high trumps or a 50 sequence.

The schmeiss is a unique feature of Klaberjass. As nondealer, schmeiss when you have only a fair chance to win with the trump proposed and fear opponent may make a big score picking a different suit for trumps. Otherwise, pass and name a good suit later.

When nondealer passes, dealer should accept or schmeiss if possible rather than allowing opponent to name a new trump suit.

If opponent is nearing 500 and you are rather behind, don't become maker unless you have a chance to win big. Otherwise opponent will score enough points simply as defender.

Variations: Some players allow nondealer a schmeiss on the second round, after two passes. For instance, "Schmeiss clubs" leaves dealer the choice to either throw the hand in or be the defender with clubs as trump. Dealer cannot schmeiss on the second round.

⊰2-10-JACK⊱

This is a quick and nifty game, with lots of little agonies and ironies. In pursuing the high-scoring cards, you might instead wind up taking high negative-scoring cards. Its name comes from the high value given to the ♥2-10-J and ♠2-10-J.

Object: To win tricks containing plus cards and to lose tricks containing minus cards.

Count of cards:

♥2, ♥10, ♥J	+10 each
♥A, ♥K, ♥Q	+ 5 each
♠2, ♠10, ♠J	-10 each
♠A, ♠K, ♠Q	- 5 each
♣A, ♣K, ♣Q, ♣J	+ 1 each
♦6	+ 1

The cards: A regular pack of 52 cards is used. Hearts are always trumps; aces are high. The ♠A is called "Speculation." It outranks all the other cards including the ♥A and may be used as trump.

To play: Deal six cards each, one at a time, and place the remaining cards face down as a stock pile.

Nondealer leads to the first trick. You must follow suit if able; otherwise you must trump. If you have no trump, play any card. A trick is won by the higher trump in it or, if it contains no trump, by the higher card of the suit that is led.

If a trump is led, the player holding Speculation has the option of playing it as the highest trump, but is not forced to play Speculation when it's the only possible trump. You may also use it to trump a club or diamond trick, and you must do so if it's your only trump. You must play Speculation on a spade lead, if it's your only spade. When leading Speculation, state whether it's a spade or a trump.

After each trick, both players take a new card from the stock, the winner of the trick drawing first. The winner of each trick leads to the next. Continue until all tricks have been taken.

Scoring: Sort the scoring cards in your tricks. Add up the plus cards and subtract the minus cards, and enter your scores accordingly. The players' combined scores must be +5, and it's easy to see why—the hearts and spades cancel each other out, leaving five cards of +1. The winner is the first player to get to +31.

Tips: 2-10-Jack is not an easy game to control. You have only six cards at once, and you don't know whether you'll be getting useful cards or dangerous cards from the stock. As usual, recalling the cards already played helps a lot, and so does counting trumps.

The best way to win the ♥2 (+10) is to void yourself of either clubs or diamonds and trump with it. If you hold Speculation (-5), it's hard to lose it. Your best chance is leading it as a spade when you think opponent is void and must trump it. Try to use Speculation to capture a plus card.

The 3 through 9 of trumps can be good or bad to have. They can protect your other hearts, but they could wind up trumping high minus cards in spades.

SOLITAIRE
Games

The reasons people like to play solitaire games are varied. Some games are pleasant time killers; others become intricate puzzles requiring deep concentration. The object of most solitaires is to arrange the cards in suit sequence by following certain rules. Elaborate patterns are sometimes used in laying out the cards, and for some games the pleasure of playing comes from building the array of cards. People with a mathematical bent can enjoy the type of solitaire in which you combine cards that add up to a certain amount.

Winning a solitaire game is not always a matter of luck. Some of the best games can be won quite often with careful, logical play. Other games come out so seldom that winning the game is a notable event.

⚜ LUCKY FOURS ⚜

This is a "lucky" solitaire because you have a very good chance to win, yet you appear to be making one sensational play after another. For this reason, have several onlookers around. Like its relatives Shamrocks and La Belle Lucie, Lucky Fours requires plenty of playing space.

The layout: Deal 13 four-card fans face up on the table, so that all cards are visable.

Object: To release the four aces and build complete sequences in suit up to the king.

Procedure: The top card or card sequence in any fan may be moved to the top of another group, in descending order and alternate colors. In the illustration on page 57, move the ◆A to a row above the fans to begin the suit foundations. Then move the ♣J to the ◆Q and move the ♣5 to the ♥6 to free up the ♠A. You can then move the ◆Q-♣J sequence to the ♠K.

When a space opens up, use any available king—or sequence headed by a king—to fill the space. Continue in this manner, freeing up new cards or play off onto the foundations, until all four of the aces have been built to kings, or until the game is blocked.

Tips: Keep making sequences at the ends of fans. This will help you to unload them later on their foundations.

When you have a choice of similar plays to make, such as two red eights to go on a black 9, look ahead to what the result of either play may bring, and choose accordingly.

❧ TUT'S TOMB ❧

Many solitaires call for adding cards together. This is a version of a widely popular solitaire called Pyramid. Here the king of spades represents King Tutankhamen of Egypt and rests atop a pyramid of cards.

The layout: Put the ♠K down first, and create a pyramid of overlapping rows as shown. The last row will have seven cards. Keep the rest of the pack as a stock.

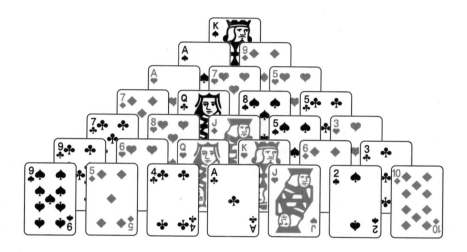

Object: To play off all the cards in pairs that add to 13. Cards have the same value as their rank. Aces count 1, jacks 11, and queens 12. Kings count 13 and are removed from the pyramid alone.

Procedure: Remove all pairs of available cards in the lay-out that total 13. At the outset, only the lowest pyramid cards are free. As cards are removed, new cards become exposed above.

59

In the layout shown on page 59, remove the 9 and 4, as well as the J and 2. Notice that at one edge this leaves a 10 with a 3 above it. Even these may be removed as a pair, since lifting the 10 frees the 3.

Turn cards from the stock, one at a time, to look for matches with available cards in the pyramid. Start a waste heap with cards that cannot be used. The top card of the waste heap stays available until it is covered. To win the game, all the cards in the pyramid and in the stock pile have to be paired off. You can go through the stock pile only once.

⊰GOOD⊱ NEIGHBORS

Pay attention to this catchy little solitaire, also known as Monte Carlo or Weddings. It may look innocent enough, but some skill is required, since you've got many choices in the play.

The layout: Deal four rows across of five cards each, face up.

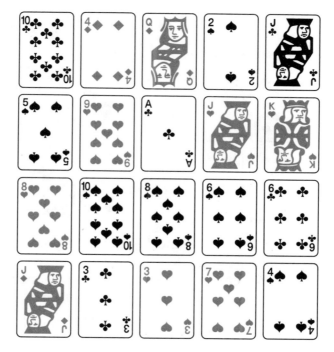

Object: To pair off and remove all the cards in the pack.

Procedure: You may remove any pair of cards of the same rank, provided they are vertical, diagonal, or horizontal

61

neighbors. In the layout shown on page 61, you'll find three such pairs: 6s, 3s and jacks. Note that the two 8s can't be taken, as they are not neighbors.

Fill the spaces of pairs taken by moving the remaining layout cards to the left, and then up and over to the end of the row above. (Spaces at the right end of a row fill from the left-hand side of the row below it.)

For example, remove 3s and Js from the layout on page 61. Move the ♠5 from the left of the second row up to the first, moving the remaining cards along so that the four spaces are at the end. Fill in those spaces with new cards from the pack as shown in the illustration above. Then look for more "good neighbors."

Continue removing pairs until the whole pack is taken. If at any turn the layout has no matches, the game is lost.

Tip: When dealing with a choice of plays, consider the various outcomes. The player in the example shown retained the 6s to have a sure match on the next turn.

⚜ KLONDIKE ⚜

Klondike is so widely known that for many people the game is synonymous with solitaire. In England the game is known as Canfield, but in the United States Canfield refers to a different solitaire. Why it has been so popular is a puzzle, since you don't end up a winner very often.

The layout: Deal a row of seven cards with the leftmost one face up and the rest face down. On top of the face-down cards, deal another row of cards, with the leftmost of these face up. Keep doing this until you have seven piles, ranging from one card on the left to seven cards on the right, with the top cards face up. The remainder of the cards form the stock.

Object: To release the four aces and build sequences in suit on them.

Procedure: As aces become available, they go into a foundation row above the layout. You can build downward sequences on the cards in the layout in alternating color only. Sequences can be moved to other piles as a unit. Top cards on the piles are available to put on the foundation piles. As cards move off their piles, turn up the card beneath. Occasionally a pile empties, opening up a vacancy. This can be filled only with a king or a sequence headed by a king.

With the tableau shown on page 64, play the ♥A into the foundation row. Then move the ♦10 onto the ♣J, and the ♠9 onto the ♦10, and move all three cards onto the ♥Q. This releases four new cards to turn over.

When the layout has no further plays, turn cards singly from the stock. Play these on the foundations or layout if possible; otherwise discard into a waste heap. The top waste-heap card remains available until another covers it. You may go through the stock only once.

63

Variations: Many favor turning the stock in bunches of three. At first this shows you only every third card, but as soon as you can use a card, then the one below it also becomes available. When the pack runs out, just turn the waste heap over and go through it in threes again. Each time through, you'll see new cards unless none was used the round before.

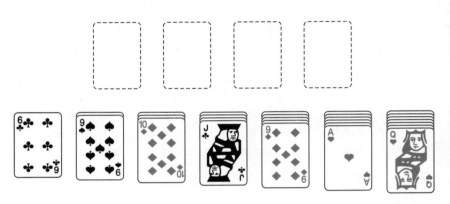

⧽FOUR CORNERS⧼

In this entertaining endeavor, each suit has its own "exclusive" corner. Once the layout gets started, only members may enter.

The layout: Distribute the four aces one to each corner, as in the illustration on page 66. Deal four cards around each ace. In the center, leave room for the rest of the pack and a waste heap.

Object: To build each suit in sequence upon its corner ace.

Procedure: Look for deuces anywhere in the layout to place on their appropriate aces. Look for the 3s that go on the 2s, etc.

In the tableau illustrated on page 66, put the ♥2 and ♥3 on the ♥A, and the ♠2 on the ♠A.

Turn over cards from the pack one at a time. Discard those that can't be played into the waste heap. Refill open corner spaces by cards of the appropriate suit only. They may come from the pack, from the top of the waste pile, or from cards in the original layout.

As the game progresses, continue building up the four suit sequences whenever possible.

Turn the waste heap over and go through the pack again. To win, you must complete each sequence this time around.

Tips: Since you have two chances to go through the pack, it's OK to leave high cards for the second time around. Try to "park" low cards in their correct corners, as well as any intermediate cards that might soon come into play.

As spaces open up, you may have several options for filling them. Usually you should try not to fill with a high card right away, unless that opens a key low card that could get trapped in the waste heap.

When several spaces are open, with no great play to make from the waste heap, it's probably better to check out the next cards from the pack.

On the second time through, try not to bury any low card in the waste heap under a higher card of the same suit. If this happens, the game will be blocked.

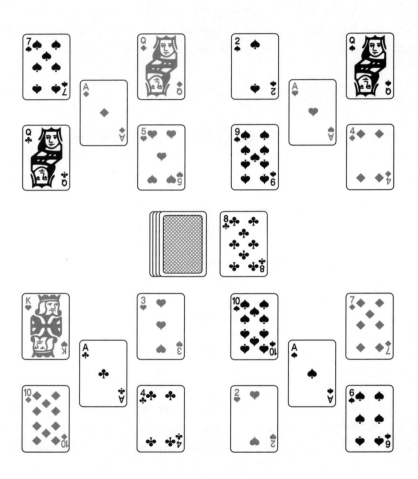

⚜ CALCULATION ⚜

One of the older solitaire games, Calculation is a favorite of players who like a pastime requiring skill and forethought. With a little practice in waste-heap management, you can win this one frequently.

The layout: Place any A, 2, 3, and 4 in a foundation column.

Object: To build on the four foundation cards in numerical sequences. Build on the ace by ones, on the 2 by twos, on the 3 by threes, and on the 4 by fours. Suit does not matter. The completed layout would look like the illustration below.

Procedure: Turn cards from the pack one by one, building on any foundation when possible. Lay off unplayable cards into one of four waste piles, as you choose. The top card of any waste pile is always available. It's customary to spread the waste heaps downward to see the cards "buried" within each. You may go through the pack only once.

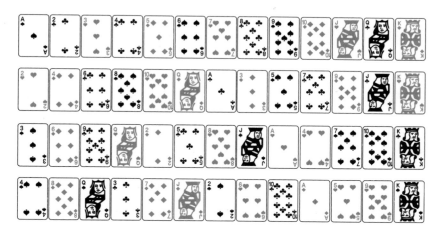

Tips: Queens, 6s and 8s are needed fairly early in the play, while 10s, jacks, and especially kings are needed later. Clever selection of card placement in the waste heaps is essential to succeed in this game. Some players save one waste heap for the kings.

When the opportunity occurs, place waste cards into heaps so that they can later play back consecutively. For example, place a 5 on a 9, and an ace on the 5, for later playback to the 4 row.

⚔ OSMOSIS ⚕

Osmosis in the outside world refers to the passing of air or liquid through a porous wall. It's not clear how this popular, luck-driven solitaire game got such a scientific name. For some mysterious reason, it's also known as Captain Kidd and Treasure Trove. You'll win at this game only a bit more often than you find buried treasure.

The layout: Deal, face down, a column of four packets of four cards each. Turn up the top card on each. Deal the next card face up and to the right of the top packet. This card, and the three others of the same rank will be—as they show up—the four foundation bases. The remaining cards form the stock.

Object: To play off cards from the stock and tableau so as to build a chain of 13 cards in each suit. These suit chains don't need to be in order.

Procedure: Across the first row, play any cards from the tableau of the same suit as the foundation card. Overlap them enough so that all cards are seen. As the top card is played from each of the piles at left, turn over the next card. The piles are not refilled when they are depleted.

Turn up cards from the pack in three-card bunches. The top card of a bunch is always available. If you play it, the card underneath is available. Unused cards go into a waste heap.

As soon as the next base-number card appears, use it to begin a second suit chain in a row underneath the first. You can now add on any card of this second suit, but only if the card of the same rank is already in the row above.

Each new row must start off with the card of the correct base number. You can join a new card to a suit chain as long

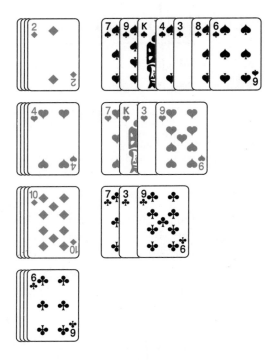

Here the base cards are 7s. Since the ♠4 has already been played in the row above, the ♥4 can be played in the hearts row. However, the ♣6 can't be played to the clubs row, because the ♥6 hasn't been played.

as the card of the same rank already appears in the suit chain just above.

Turn the waste heap over each time you've gone through the pack. Play on until the game is won or (more likely) blocked.

Variation: Since a blockage in any tableau pile will doom the game, some players follow the variant called Peek. The four piles are dealt face up to show their contents. This permits you to see a hopeless blockage and lets you abandon the deal.

⤙CANFIELD⤚

Canfield is named after the owner of a celebrated gaming house in Sarasota Springs, New York. Mr. Canfield sold a pack of cards for $50 and paid the player $5 for every card played onto the foundation cards. Undoubtedly this venture did not lose him money.

The layout: Deal a packet of 13 cards face down. Turn it face up and set it at the left for a reserve pile. Deal another card face up above and to the right of the reserve pile. This is the first of four foundation cards. As other cards of the same rank become available, add them onto this row.

Just beneath the foundation row, deal a row of four cards to start the tableau.

Object: To build four ascending suit sequences, each beginning with the base-number card. The suits are built around the corner: Ace follows king and deuce follows ace.

Procedure: Deal cards from the pack in threes, placing cards not used on a single face-up waste pile. The uppermost card on the waste pile remains an available card.

Add to the foundations with cards from the pack, the reserve, the tableau, or the waste heap. You may build downward sequences, alternating in color, from the tableau cards. These sequences can be built around the corner like the ascending sequences: A king can be played on an ace. You may also move an entire sequence of tableau cards onto another, creating a longer sequence, in order to clear a space. Spaces are filled with a card from the reserve pile. If the reserve pile is used up, fill open tableau spaces with available cards from the pack or waste heap.

Turn up cards from the pack in three-card bunches. The top card of a bunch is always available. If you play it, the card underneath is available. Put unused cards into a waste heap, the top card of which is available.

Turn the waste heap over each time you've gone through the pack. Keep on until the game is won or you can make no more plays.

Variation: A slight variant called Storehouse makes things a little easier for you. Always remove the four deuces in advance and use them as the foundation-row base cards. Then build on each deuce upward in suit to the ace.

ꕔACCORDIONꕔ

Even if you're not musical, you can while away idle moments playing the popular pastime Accordion. Each game is quick and requires only a small space. However, the solitaire hardly ever comes out.

The layout: Simply keep dealing out cards in a row.

Object: To form a single face-up pile of all the cards.

Procedure: As you deal cards into a single row, pile cards onto other cards to the left according to two rules of matching: (1) The two cards must be either the same suit or the same rank, and (2) the cards must be either next to each other or have two cards between.

Pile matches together onto the card on the left. Then treat any pile made as a single card. Look to see if one move has created another. If you have no more moves, play a new card at the end of a row.

Occasionally a newly turned card gives two possible moves; you may make either. The game ends in a single pile very rarely; you're doing very well to get down to just two or three piles.

Dealing the ♠3 gives you your first move. The ♠3 can be piled onto its match, the ♥3 (same rank). The ♠3 now matches the ♠7 (same suit) directly on its left, so the two-card pile can be moved onto the ♠7. Since no matches remain, continue by adding a new card to the end of the row.

Variations: Start by dealing a 13-card row, which will probably give you choices of moves to make. Before playing, you may enjoy trying to project their different results. When you've made all your moves, add new cards to the row until 13 are again showing and proceed as before.

A similar solitaire is called Royal Wedding. Start by placing the ♥Q on the top of the pack and the ♥K on the bottom. Deal out the pack one card at a time, starting with the ♥Q. As you proceed, throw out single cards and pairs of cards that stand between cards that match by suit or rank. You win the game if you wind up with just the ♥Q and ♥K, the Royal Marriage. It won't happen very often.

⇥GAPS⇤

This widely known solitaire gives you a chance to put on your thinking cap. The name comes from the gaps left in the layout once play begins. Blue Moon and Spaces are among other names given to this interesting, mazelike exercise.

The layout: Deal out the whole deck in four rows of 13 cards. Then take the four aces out of the layout and put them aside.

Object: To end up with four 12-card rows, each one should be a complete suit in sequence from 2 through king.

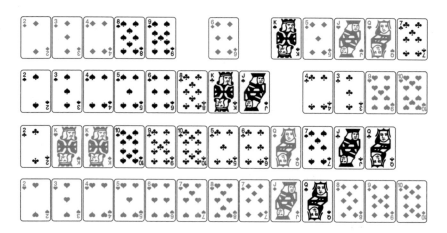

Move the ♦7 to the space to the right of the ♦6. This opens up the space for the next card in the hearts row. Moving the ♠10 to the space to the right of the ♠9 creates a block after the ♦K.

Procedure: You may fill any space with the next higher card to the card at the left of that space. For example, if a space lies to the right of the ♣10, take the ♣J from its pres-

*The game after the unmatched cards were redealt and the aces
were removed.*

ent position and fill that space. This will leave a new space
where the ♣J was.

Fill an empty space at the left end of a row with any
deuce. A space behind a king cannot be filled. But if you're
able to move that king behind its proper queen, the space
may open up again.

When all four gaps are behind kings, card movement is
blocked. Gather up all cards in the layout that aren't in their
correct sequence behind deuces. Shuffle up these cards and
the four aces, then deal the cards to fill out the four 13-card
rows. Remove the aces as before and proceed with the play.
If this layout gets stalled too, you're allowed one further redeal.

Tips: Usually three or four plays are possible at the start
of a game, each opening up a series of further moves. You
may see that some plays will soon lead to a useless space behind a king. To follow each line of play can be perplexing at
first, but you'll get better at it after playing a few times.

It helps to identify a card you would like to move and
work back to see what other cards need to move before you
can move that card.

Variations: A number of players handle the redeals by omitting the aces and leaving a gap in each row behind the last correctly positioned card. If a row has not yet been started, leave a gap at the left, for a deuce.

GAPS FOR TWO: Gaps can be played as an interesting, though heady, competition for two. One player shuffles and deals a layout. The other then sets up an exact replica layout with another deck. There's no redeal; whoever can get more cards into proper suit sequence is the winner.

⊰POKER SOLITAIRE⊱

Poker Solitaire lets you play up to 12 Poker hands at once, and you can keep score to see how well you're doing. It can also be played by two.

The layout: Place 25 cards one by one into a face-up grid of five columns and five rows.

Object: To arrange the 25 cards into high-scoring five-card poker combinations.

Royal flush	*Straight flush*	*Four of a kind*
Full house	*Flush*	*Straight*
Three of a kind	*Two pair*	*One pair*

Procedure: Shuffle the pack and turn up cards one at a time. Place each card within the framework of an imaginary five-by-five square of cards. Once you place a card, you can't move it. After you've played all 25 cards, tally your score. Total up twelve poker hands: the five columns, the five rows, and the two diagonals. A good score is 200.

Scoring:

Royal flush	100
Straight flush	75
Four of a kind	50
Full house	25
Flush	20
Straight	15
Three of a kind	10
Two pair	5
One pair	2

The scoring table above is the American version, which considers the likihood of getting that hand in actual poker.

Tips: You'll increase your chances of making straights if you avoid putting an ace, 2, queen, or king in the center of the grid.

Don't plan on lots of straight flushes, but leave some chances open early in the play. Just don't wait too long to convert three cards held for a straight flush into a possible straight hand or flush hand.

Variations: Some players do not count the two diagonal hands.

As a two-player game, one player deals out the 25 cards, and the other player duplicates them with a separate deck. Each completes an independent card arrangement, in sight of each other if they wish. The location of each player's five-by-five framework should be determined at the outset. One way to assure this is to require that the first card be played in the center.

⚐FORTY THIEVES ⚐

This challenging solitaire is also called Napoleon at St. Helena's and Big Forty. Skillful play pays off. If you pay close attention and plan your moves carefully, you can win this one reasonably often.

The layout: Shuffle two 52-card decks together. Deal out a row of ten cards face up. Overlapping them slightly, deal another row of ten cards over the first row. Continue until 40 cards have been dealt in four rows. Above these, leave room for eight foundations. See the illustrated layout on page 81.

Object: To build suit sequences on all eight aces up to the king.

Procedure: As aces are released, place them above the layout as foundations. The bottom card of each column is available and may be played in downward suit sequence onto another available card or in upward suit sequence on a foundation pile. In the illustration, once the ♥A is moved into the foundation area you can move the ♣10 onto the ♣J. Cards in the layout can be moved only one card at a time. You can't move the ♣10 and the ♣J as a unit onto the ♣Q, should that become available.

Turn cards up from the stock one at a time. Cards that cannot be played to the tableau or foundations form a single waste heap, whose top card is always available. You can go through the pack only once.

When all the cards in a column have been played, fill the space left behind by any playable card.

Tips: Success is likely to rest with your ability to clear out one or more columns. With one or two spaces available for transportation, you can maneuver longer card sequences.

Variations: Some players allow tableau sequences to stack downward in alternating suit color. Although this does not keep the suits together, it offers twice as many possible plays and will increase your odds of winning.

Another way to boost your chances is to place the eight aces into the foundation row and then deal out the "40 Thieves" below.

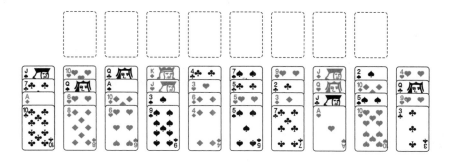

⊰SPIDER⊱

This tough solitaire appeals to those who seek a formidable challenge. To conquer it, good judgment must combine with better luck. Franklin D. Roosevelt found it his own favorite solitaire. You too may find yourself caught up for quite a while in the Spider's web before winning your way out.

The layout: Shuffle together two 52-card packs. Deal a row of ten cards face down. Deal three more rows of ten cards face down on top of the first row. Deal an additional card to the each of the first four piles. Then lay a card face up on each of the ten piles. Hold the remaining 50 cards aside as a stock. The tableau should look like the illustration on page 83.

Object: To form within the layout eight suit sequences in downward order from king to ace. Sequences thus formed are taken out of the layout.

Procedure: All the action is within the tableau. You may play an upcard onto any card one rank above it, regardless of suit. You can move as a unit a sequence of cards in the same suit. Otherwise cards move singly. No card can be played onto an ace. A king or sequence headed by a king can move only into an empty space.

Whenever a face-down card is uncovered, turn it up. When a pile empties, fill its space with any available card or natural sequence.

When you run out of moves, or choose to make no new ones, deal another row of ten cards face up onto the layout. First you must fill in any spaces in the layout. When the whole new row is in place, you can continue playing.

Whenever you produce an entire suit sequence, you may remove it from play immediately. Or you may keep it in play if breaking it up can keep the game alive.

Tips: On the original deal, you want to get as many face-down cards uncovered as you can. Move cards onto cards of the same suit if possible. If such a move is not available, move top-ranking cards first. In the example shown below, move the ◆6 onto the ◆7 first. You might turn up a useful card under the ◆6. If not, move the ◆10 onto the ♥J before playing the ♣9 onto the ◆10.

Each new row of ten cards is a mixed blessing—you get ten new cards to deal with, but they block all the work done so far.

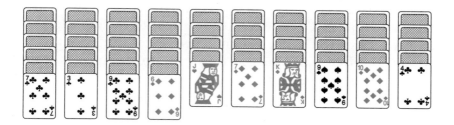

⚘ PROPELLER ⚘

Also called The Windmill, this attractive solitaire can be won often, with attentive play. The name comes from the Propeller's "wings," which appear to spin around on the tableau.

The layout: Shuffle two 52-card decks together. Take any ace from the pack and place it in the center of the layout. Place two cards face up in a line above the ace and two cards face up below it. Place two cards in a row to the ace's left and two cards to the ace's right. These eight cards are the wings. The first four kings, as they turn up, go in each of the four positions diagonal to the ace.

Object: To build four successive ace-to-king sequences in a single pile upon the center ace, and one downward king-to-ace sequence on each of the four king foundations. The sequences are built without regard to suit.

Procedure: Deal the cards from the pack one by one; either play them on one of the five foundations or discard them into a single waste pile. The top card of the waste pile can be played onto a foundation. The cards in the wings are also available to be played. Refill spaces in the wings with cards from either the waste pile or the stock.

You're allowed to remove a card from a king-to-ace foundation to put on the center foundation, but only once at a time. Your next play to the center has to be from the pack, the wings, or the waste pile.

Keep going until both packs play out onto the foundations or until the pack has been dealt out and the game is blocked. No redeal is allowed in this game.

Here is the layout from page 84 further along in the game. You can play the ♠7 on the center ♦6. This allows you to play the ♥8.

⊰GRANDFATHER'S⊱ CLOCK

This rousing solitaire is sure to keep you ticking. Play your cards right and bide your time—and you'll wind up with a picture-perfect finish. A nostalgic relic, Grandfather's Clock is also known as Clock Solitaire. No matter what you call it, it's "hour" favorite!

The layout: From a double deck, select 2-6-10 of one suit, 3-7-J of another, 4-8-Q of a third suit, and 5-9-K of the fourth suit. Arrange them in numerical order as in the face of a clock, with the 6 placed at one o'clock (see diagram on page 87). These 12 cards are the foundations.

Next deal three circles of 12 cards each face up and overlapping around the outside of the clock face, as shown. These are reserves. The remaining cards form the stock.

Object: To build upward suit sequences on each foundation card, aces following kings. When the game is won, all cards have been played out and an ace sits at one o'clock, a deuce is at two o'clock, a trey at three o'clock, and so on, with a jack at 11 o'clock and a queen at 12 o'clock.

Procedure: Turn cards from the stock one by one, going through the pack just one time. Discards go into a single waste heap, whose top card is always available. On the tableau, only the outermost reserve cards are available. A card played will release the one beneath it.

You may build onto the foundation piles from the reserves, the stock, or the waste heap. In the layout shown, build the ♦Q onto the foundation ♦J at six o'clock.

Play onto available reserve cards in downward suit sequence. In the example shown on page 87, you start by

86

moving the ♥10 onto the ♥J, the ♣4 onto the ♣5 and both onto the ♣6. The ♥5 then released may be moved onto the ♥4 in the clock. You may move as a single unit a group of cards all connected in downward suit sequence.

When any reserve pile has fewer than three cards, fill its available slots only from the unseen stock and never from the waste heap or from other reserves.

Tips: You can win Grandfather's Clock fairly often if you make the most sensible plays and watch what's going on. Often you'll have quite a few plays and sometimes even a choice of plays between identical cards. Look to see which cards would be released by each alternative.

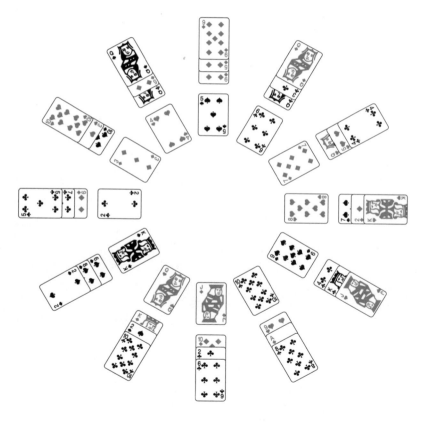

⚔ THE SNAKE ⚔

This unusual solitaire is suspenseful to play and leaves a pleasing picture.
Although it's very easy to win this game, you'll find it an
absorbing pastime.

The layout: Shuffle two 52-card packs together. Arrange any 13 sequential cards, beginning with a 7, into a Z-shaped tableau.

Object: To build eight-card sequences on each of the 13 foundation cards in the tableau. When successful, the complete pack will be played out, with the cards showing in value from the ace through the king.

Procedure: Deal cards up one by one and play in upward sequence on foundations whenever possible. Suit does not matter in this game. Cards turned that cannot be played are deposited in either of two waste heaps. The top card of each waste heap remains available for play and reveals the card beneath if played. No moves between waste heaps are permitted.

Tips: Skill in placing cards onto the two waste piles is what really makes a difference. For example, an 8 that is placed on a 9 in the waste pile is usually a good play, because if the 8 plays later, so can the 9. You should try to avoid placing cards in ascending order for this reason. However, since there are many playoff piles, such a play might not be fatal.

This is the Z-shaped starting layout for The Snake. Seven cards played in order on the 7, making a pile of eight, will have a top card of ace.

❧MISS MILLIGAN❧

Whoever she was, Miss Milligan has given her name to one of the most popular of the double-deck solitaire games. It's similar to Spider in that successive deals cover up the work you've done.

The layout: Shuffle two 52-card decks together. Deal out a row of eight cards face up.

Object: To build suit sequences on the eight aces, which as they become available are placed above the row of eight cards.

Procedure: First move up any aces to the foundation row. The eight cards can be played onto each other in downward sequences of alternating colors. A sequence can be moved as a unit. Vacancies can be filled only by a king or a sequence of cards headed by a king. When you've made all the moves that you can, deal another eight cards face up overlapping the first row of cards and filling in any holes in the layout as you go.

After you have dealt out all the cards, a unique feature called weaving comes into play. You have the option of removing one card or sequence from the layout and setting it aside in order to play the card underneath it. If later you are able to build this card or sequence back onto the layout or onto the foundation, you can set aside another card or sequence.

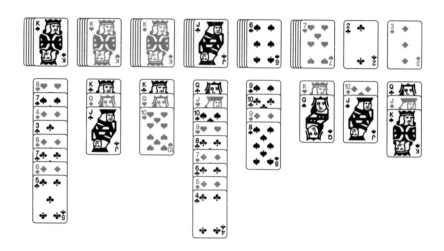

Although the ♣3 is blocked, you can temporarily move ◆8-♣7-◆6-♣5 aside to play the cards underneath.

❧ THE SULTAN OF ❧ TURKEY

The most delightful feature of this solitaire is the pattern it creates when you win, which is more often than not. You'll be treated to a view of the Sultan—the king of hearts—surrounded by his harem of eight queens.

The layout: From a double deck, remove the eight kings and one ace. Arrange them in three rows of three, with a king of hearts in the center and the ace underneath it. The cards surrounding the king of hearts are the foundations.

Add a column of four cards on each side of this array. These cards are available to play on the foundations. The remaining cards form the stock.

Object: To build suit sequences from ace to queen on the seven outside kings and from deuce to queen on the ace. The central king of hearts is not built on.

Procedure: Deal cards from the stock one by one, playing them either on the foundations or to a single waste pile. The top card of the waste pile is available for play, as are the cards from the two side columns, onto the foundations. Vacancies in the columns are filled from the waste pile or the stock. You are allowed two redeals, which is usually enough to make the game come out.

GLOSSARY

Bella. In Klaberjass, the king and queen of trumps.

Bid. A spoken declaration to win a specified number of tricks or points; to make such a declaration.

Big Casino. In Casino, the ten of diamonds.

Blucher. In Nap, one of three bids to take five tricks.

Build. In Casino, to combine two or more cards so they can be taken with another card; also, the combination itself.

Canasta. In Canasta, a natural canasta is a meld of seven cards of the same rank. In a mixed canasta, from one to three cards are replaced by wild cards.

Crib. In Cribbage, the extra hand, belonging to the dealer, formed by the players' discards.

Deadwood. In Gin Rummy, unmatched cards in a hand.

Deal. The act of portioning out the cards to the players; also, the period of play in the game between one deal and the next.

Deuce. A card of the rank of two; a two-spot.

Dix. In Pinochle, the lowest trump.

Draw trumps. To lead high trump cards in order to deplete opponent's hand of trumps.

Face card. A jack, queen, or king (not an ace).

Flush. A set of cards all of the same suit.

Follow suit. To play a card of the suit that was led.

Foundation. In solitaire, a starting card on which specific other cards are played.

Full house. In Poker, a hand with three of a kind and a pair.

Gin. In Gin Rummy, a hand completely matched in melding sets, with no deadwood.

Hand. The cards dealt to a player; also, the period of play in the game between one deal and the next.

Jass. In Klaberjass, the jack of trump.

Knock. In Rummy and Gin Rummy, to end play by laying down a hand that is not completely matched.

Lead. To play the first card of a trick.

Left bower. In Euchre, the jack of the same color as the trump suit.

Little Casino. In Casino, the two of spades.

Maker. A player who takes on a specific obligation, such as to take a certain number of points or tricks, often along with the right to choose the trump suit.

Marriage. A meld consisting of the king and queen of a suit.

Meld. A combination of cards with scoring value; to show or play such a combination.

Menel. In Klaberjass, the 9 of trump.

Misère. In Nap, a bid of three no trump.

Napoleon. In Nap, one of three bids to take five tricks.

Pass. A spoken declaration not to make a bid.

Peg. In Cribbage, to score points.

Quartet. In Cribbage, four cards of the same rank.

Reserve. In solitaire, a group of cards available to be played.

Right bower. In Euchre, the jack of the trump suit.

Royal flush. In Poker, an ace-high straight flush.

Schmeiss. In Klaberjass, a proposal to either accept the upcard as trump or throw in the deal.

Singleton. A holding of only one card in a suit.

Speculation. In 2-10-Jack, the ace of spades, which is the highest-ranking card.

Stock. The undealt cards available for future use.

Straight. In Poker, five cards in sequence but not in the same suit.

Straight flush. In Poker, five cards in sequence and in the same suit.

Tableau. In solitaire, the layout of cards on the playing surface, not including the foundations.

Trail. In Casino, to play a card without building on or taking in other cards.

Trey. A card of the rank of three; a three-spot.

Trick. A round of cards played, one from each player's hand.

Triplet. In Cribbage, three cards of the same rank.

Trump. A suit designated to be higher-ranking than any other suit; any card in that suit. Also, to play a trump card on a trick.

Undercut. In Gin Rummy, to show a hand with deadwood counting less than or equal to the knocker's hand.

Upcard. The first card turned face up after the deal.

Void. A holding of no cards in a particular suit.

Wellington. In Nap, one of three bids to take five tricks.

Wild card. A card that can be designated by the holder as being any other card.